THE ART OF SUCKER DUCKIN

Tierre Caldwell

THE ART OF SUCKER DUCKIN

Before you read this book close your eyes and ask God to remove anybody and anything that doesn't belong in your life… don't be surprised if in a short time you have fewer friends, become single, or undergo some type of personal change; it's all God doing Him!

TABLE OF CONTENTS

The Art Of Sucker Duckin	**vii**
Chapter One: The Suckers' Nature	**1**
The 5 Rules Of A Suckers' Nature	1
The Bait Suckers Use To Provoke And Deceive	3
Necessary Illusion	5
Sucker Situations	6
How To Coexist With Suckers	6
Action Plan	**8**
Chapter Two: The Sickness & Unclean Spirits	**9**
What Are Unclean Spirits?	9
What Are Their Objectives?	10
The Different Types Of Spirits	10
The Sickness	11
The 10 Deadly Plagues Of The Sickness And How They Destroy Your Life	12
Action Plan	**17**
Chapter Three: The Circle Of Limitation	**19**
1st Dimension: Individuals	20
2nd Dimension: Environment	23
3rd Dimension: Consequences	25
Action Plan	**28**

Chapter Four: The Psychology Of Purpose	**29**
The Fear Of Identity	29
The Separation Of Self	30
No True Knowledge Of Self	30
Never Discovering Your Purpose	31
How Long Will You Run From Your Purpose?	31
That Gorilla Suit Doesn't Fit You!	33
Codependency	36
Action Plan	**37**
Chapter Five: Suckerizm	**38**
The Four Traps Of Suckerizm	38
The Culture Of Suckerizm	39
The Miseducation Of Suckerizm	40
The Seduction Of Suckerizm	41
The Addiction Of Suckerizm	43
Action Plan	**46**
Chapter Six: How To Be Sucker Free In 4 Stages	**47**
Why Boundaries Are So Important To Purpose?	48
How To Set Boundaries And Enforce Them	48
Types Of Boundaries	49
What Do Boundaries Sound Like?	50
The Trauma Of Wasted Energy	51

The Devil And Wasted Energy	52
How Do You Monitor Your Energy And Maneuver Past The Attacks?	54
The Struggle Between The Two Natures In The Relapse Stage	55
So Why Am I Stuck Between Who I *Used To* Be And Who I *Know* God Called Me To Be?	57
What is The Key To Life, Self, and Purpose?	62
Action Plan	**63**
Chapter Seven: How Women Can Be Sucker Free In Relationships	**65**
A Message To Women Who Keep Dating Suckers	69
Ladies - How Do You Spot A Man Who's A Sucker?	71
Action Plan	**72**
Chapter Eight: Think Legacy, Speak Destiny, Glorify Your Creator	**73**
Think Legacy	73
Speak Destiny	74
Glorify Your Creator	74
Action Plan	**75**
Chapter Nine: How To Build A Circle Of Elevation	**77**
The Nucleus	77

The Inner-Circle	78
The Outer-Circle	80
The Circumference	81
Action Plan	83
The Art Of Sucker Duckin By: Tierre Caldwell	84
About The Author	85

THE ART OF SUCKER DUCKIN

Sucker Duckin by definition is to disassociate yourself from any situation, relationship, or affiliation that limits the growth of life, self, or purpose.

The word **SUCKER** is an acronym that stands for **S**omeone **U**ltimately **C**onspiring to **K**ill **E**verything **R**ighteous. The word **DUCKIN** stands for **D**emonstrating an **U**nderstanding of **C**onscious **K**nowledge **I**mmune to **N**othingness.

You may be wondering what exactly nothingness is. Nothingness is the wasted energy, emotion, talent, time, money, or relationships that block you from discovering your true potential.

Many of us are smart and talented, but the people we surround ourselves with do not always bring that out of us. Surrounding ourselves with the wrong crowd causes us to suppress our intelligence and ignore our gifts. The Art of Sucker Duckin teaches you to surround yourself with people that bring out the best in you, and duck those who bring out the worst.

What is the purpose of Duckin Suckers? The purpose of this journey is to stop allowing people to trick your life off. To help you establish the proper boundaries for who can and can not enter your life.

What are personal boundaries? They are guidelines, rules or limits that you create to identify reasonable, and safe ways for other people to behave towards you. As well as, how you will respond when someone oversteps those boundaries.

Once you learn the Art of Sucker Duckin you will have the proper boundaries established to help you:

- Live sucker free
- Keep you out of prison
- Identify unhealthy relationships
- Stay alive
- Put you on the path to success
- Help you realize your true potential in life

You will learn how to keep all relationships, personal and professional, sucker free. I will help you develop a sucker free spirit and even confront the sucker within you. Then you will be able to duck the biggest sucker of all, the Devil.

Chapter One

THE SUCKER'S NATURE

The sucker's nature examines a sucker's method of operation; how easily they can sabotage and why. While the entire world is focused on haters hating from afar, suckers have flown completely under the radar unnoticed. They operate using protocols of sabotage and destroy your life from the inside out. Why? Because they are staying true to their nature. Suckers are so crafty and conniving, they point out haters with you. By the end of this chapter, you will learn how to identify a sucker with ease.

The 5 Rules Of a Suckers' Nature

Rule 1: Understand that it is not in the suckers' nature to hate you as an individual--that is what haters do. Suckers hate what you represent, and it is wise to not take anything they say or do personal.

An emotional reaction to an ignorant outburst is always wasted energy.

Remember, suckers always attack what they lack so it is not what is wrong with you, it is what is not right with them.

Rule 2: Understand that suckers are natural enemies of power, respect, charisma, stability, righteousness, and success. They harbor a deep-rooted level of resentment toward those who are comfortable with themselves, or who possess more than what they do.

The foundation of a sucker's dominant character attributes are centered around three things: nothingness, manipulation, and sabotage.

Rule 3: Suckers are suicide bombers--they don't care about their own health, safety, reputation, freedom, or children. They will risk it all just to ruin what you have built.

Remember, their only mission is to stop you from completing yours. If your job is to build, theirs is to destroy.

Rule 4: Know the difference between suckers and haters. Haters like to stay a safe distance away from you to hate you; but they do not get too close. Suckers will get to know you, spend time with you, study you, rehearse your weaknesses, then at the moment you are set to cultivate whatever it is you deem righteous, they will sabotage it.

Remember this; a hater won't give their life to stop you, a sucker will.

Hate is fear turned backward. That's why haters do not get close, they fear what they do not understand. Suckers do not fear you, they fear what you are capable of. They only want to understand why they hate themselves. That confusion is their justified solution to hate everything you personify.

Notice: suckers will approach you with a seemingly harmless and over interested attitude. They will portray an authentic larger-than-life type of aura of themselves to appear as if they are above anything petty in life or in thought.

<u>Rule 5:</u> Suckers are masters of **<u>nothingness.</u>** To sucker duck effectively, you must practice identifying, reducing, and eliminating any and all signs of it. This is what makes a *sucker's nature* so critical to being exposed. From the definition, it seems difficult to spot a sucker. How can you spot a sucker? How do you spot a man or a woman who is the sucker in a relationship? Have you been a sucker without knowing? Let's go deeper.

A clear giveaway on how to spot a sucker is that they will always try too hard to convince you of who they want you to think they are.

The sucker's appetite for identity is only satisfied by them living through your life vicariously. Suckers will probe into your personal being to learn your fears, desires, and what drives you so they can align their entire style and personality to run parallel to yours. They do this so they can create what is called the necessary illusion; which we explore shortly.

The Bait Suckers Use To Provoke And Deceive

Suckers who have not figured out how to get close enough to you and penetrate your inner circle will most likely bait you from the outside in by provoking/driving you.

Suckers provoke/drive you by putting a steering wheel on your back and steering you to destruction. They push you to

the point you flip out and destroy yourself, someone else, or something you have deemed valuable.

Remember a sucker will never care about any repercussions that stem from them trying to get a reaction out of you. They will take the beatings and any type of pain and suffering that comes from you retaliating. That is the point; they derive pleasure from pain. As long as you destroyed whatever you had going on then, the sucker won. Their happiness can only be gained by witnessing you lose something out of anger at the hands of fake energy appearing real. That is what it means when someone drives you.

Suckers by nature are often imprisoned by two things: what they **lack** and the **things they can't control.**

After being imprisoned for what they lack and what they can not control, they begin to turn the prison bars into a barricade that blocks them from growth, finding self, and discovering purpose.

Remember the one who has no self-control over his reactions will never have any safety in life.

The bait suckers use to deceive:

The bait used to deceive is 1,000 times more deadly because if you are falling for it, they have already penetrated your circle and gotten close to you.

After having a sucker around you for a long period of time, you will eventually end up finding a use for them. Beware of a favor from a traitor.

THE ART OF SUCKER DUCKIN

Once you have found a use for a sucker, the temporary benefit will blind you from their true purpose and you bypass evaluating their level of authenticity. This just means you ignore their character and focus more on what you are using them for--a common mistake.

The bait a sucker uses to deceive can come in the form of drugs, women, money, transportation, love, sex, shelter, attention, or something so simple as ego-stroking.

The bait can come in the form of any void they offered to fill and you allowed. The bait is the active ingredient in the suckers necessary illusion. Don't forget that! Suckers will also use more sophisticated forms of bait like offering favors in times of need, connections, or a network that can take you to the next level. Do not accept them. When you accept a gift in the form of a bribe you just created a self-inflicted security breach and have given the sucker the <u>access</u> they crave.

Necessary Illusion

The necessary illusion is a temporary persona or facade tailor-made by the sucker to suppress who they really are in order to gain access into specific circles, relationships, or situations for the purposes of sabotage and manipulation.

Once you have been fooled by the false image and lifestyle the sucker is portraying, the sucker sees you as careless and begins to sabotage.

The sucker will automatically begin to plot on how to capitalize on your vulnerabilities so they can destroy whatever you deem righteous. Suckers by nature have no true knowledge of *self*, that is why it is easy for them to masquerade through life as someone else. That persona is called the "necessary illusion".

Sucker Situations

Sucker situations are situations that suckers create and drag you into to waste your time, energy, emotion, freedom, or money.

Suckers prey on sympathy and poor attention to detail. They will always try to bring you into their drama. If you don't pay attention to them and allow them to fly under your wing they will begin presenting you with their baggage (problems or issues). You may feel obligated to aid and assist them because you used them for your own benefit. Suckers will have you in compromising positions that may cost you your freedom, or worse: your life.

Suckers will go to the extreme of smiling in your face, helping you out, stealing your identity, setting you up, shooting at you, then filing a restraining order on you, and snitching on you if you retaliate! Crazy, right? That is why sucker duckin is an art.

How To Coexist With Suckers

The beginning of coexistence is becoming tolerant of suckers who articulate thought and exercise behavior foreign to how you do while simultaneously keeping your emotions idle for the sake of your own peace of mind. You must first alter your understanding of people in a holistic type of way by patiently becoming receptive towards different personalities. You do this by first realizing that everybody does not think and act the same as you. Stop only entertaining people who agree with you and learn how to absorb people that will challenge you in a way that benefits them, but does not compromise your mental stability. Let people be who they are separate from who you are.

The cloth someone is cut from dictates the type of behavior you expect from them. You waste energy when you expect a sucker to go against their own nature and behave like they are cut from your strand of fabric when they are not. Let a sucker be who they are; if you won't go against your nature, why should they?

Many people feel threatened when they feel misunderstood, so the deeper understanding comes when you draw from them the empathetic connection they need to be who it is they *think* they are, and still be understood without fear of judgment or harm to their ego. If you do get upset, learn how to channel it in a different way. You must begin the practice of using your anger as an indicator to counterbalance the preservation of whatever objective you wish to achieve.

Remember that the only way to be emotionally absent amongst suckers is to be one with self.

Learn how to coexist when you are forced to be around suckers, or you will never be successful in life. To co-exist effectively you not only need to know yourself, but you need to know and understand your anger and what triggers it. What provokes it? Is it when someone insults your intelligence? Unmet expectations, being lied to, or hypocrisy?

Suckers use the very tone of anger while communicating as a self-defense mechanism to protect that *necessary illusion*

from dealing with the feelings of powerlessness, insecurities, and inferiorities.

<u>Takeaways</u>

- ⌘ You know the difference between suckers and haters.
- ⌘ You know the bait suckers use to deceive.
- ⌘ You know how to spot sucker situations.
- ⌘ You know what the "necessary illusion" looks like.
- ⌘ How to coexist with suckers.
- ⌘ Does anyone in your life fit this category? If so, who are they? Do you fit this category?
- ⌘ Do these people make you better or worse?

ACTION PLAN

Practice allowing suckers to be suckers. While you continue to strive to become a better you. Let them do what they do, however they do it. Identify all the suckers in your life and take small steps to differentiate your life from theirs. A sucker's path is not a leader's lane. If you value your freedom and stability you will begin to diversify your circle expeditiously.

Chapter Two

THE SICKNESS & UNCLEAN SPIRITS

Suckers are parasites that carry unclean spirits within them. They are attracted to the glow of righteous energy. Once you invite a sucker into your inner circle, you also invite those same energies into your life. Once they have been around you for so long, they will transfer these same unclean spirits to you and your circumstances; this creates the sickness and destroys your life.

Here, the Art of Sucker Duckin (ASD) teaches what unclean spirits are, their objectives, the different types, what areas of your life they can infect, and how you can tell if you have caught the sickness.

What are unclean spirits?

Unclean spirits are demonic entities minus a physical body. These spirits come from the author of all evil; Satan. If you think the devil can't attack your mind through other people you are wrong. These unclean spirits move in unison as a well-organized army with the intent to plague your mind. When you have negative self-sabotaging thoughts that are not your own and you believe them and act on them you have been affected by an unclean spirit.

What are their objectives?

- Seduce
- Corrupt
- Enslave
- Coerce
- Mislead
- Steal
- Kill
- Destroy

The different types of spirits

1. The spirit of negativity
2. The spirit of bitterness
3. The spirit of fear
4. The spirit of violence
5. The spirit of resentment
6. The spirit of abandonment
7. The spirit of lust
8. The spirit of hate
9. The spirit of addiction
10. The spirit of envy

If evil spirits are unable to possess you, they attempt to manipulate you. If you can not identify spirits in other people you may end up in a toxic relationship with a sucker thus causing you to be at war with that person's spirit. This is not the persons doing but it is actually a spiritual sickness. If you are not careful, you subconsciously begin to develop some of those same characteristics as those around you after a while.

The Sickness

WHAT ARE THE SYMPTOMS OF THE SICKNESS?

- You focus more on your limitations than capabilities.
- You listen to the voice in your head that speaks doubt.
- You worry more than you pray.
- You become anti-social, emotionally insensitive, selfish and passive-aggressive.
- You become extremely manipulative toward the people trying to help you in life.
- Your outlook is pessimistic and feelings are numb.
- You become indecisive and get used to rejection.
- You take your anger out on everything but the actual source of where your anger is coming from.
- You cling to gossip and the slandering of other people.
- You begin to develop resentment towards anybody who seems stable.

The sickness kills you spiritually. If you were at any point in your life spiritual, it gradually destroys your belief in that higher power. Your bitterness turns towards everyone, even God. You begin to blame him for all that is not right in your life.

The sickness annihilates your competence to the point that you only feel comfortable around people who are doing worse than you are.

Whatever harmful habit you were addicted to increases dramatically like drinking, smoking, pills, overeating, over-shopping, gambling, illegal hustling, etc.

The sickness creates a number of unhealthy coping mechanisms to assist in dealing with the loss of drive, identity, peace of mind and emptiness. You could display unhealthy submissiveness and dependence. You could confuse pity with love.

You will shy away from intimacy. You will create different personalities or hide behind a wall made of the tough exterior to ease the pain.

The sickness also places self-imposed limits on your progress and overall sense of vision because you cannot see past your circle of limitation.

The sickness also creates a false sense of loyalty to the circle of people in the lifestyle who simply don't grow you in any way shape or form. Once the sickness has taken its toll this far, it evolves into a virus and makes way for the 10 plagues.

The 10 deadly plagues of the sickness and how they destroy your life

1. Routine

What happens when your routine is plagued:

- You start to neglect things.
- You miss work.
- You hustle backwards.
- You become a liability instead of an asset.
- You have no plans or routine and when you have no plans of your own you ultimately become part of someone else's.

THE ART OF SUCKER DUCKIN

You slowly coast toward rock bottom and on your way there you gravitate toward other suckers who are also doing nothing because you do not feel threatened by that level of success or status.

One becomes a critic when one cannot be an artist just as a man becomes a stool pigeon when he can't be a soldier.

-GUSTAVE FLAUBERT

2. Progress

- You are less motivated to succeed because no one around you pushes you to make it.
- You get used to doing the bare minimum or nothing.
- Your ambition is gone and your success is at a standstill so you begin to envy those who are making progress in their lives.
- You put more energy into hating what the next person has accomplished than the amount you put into achieving your goals.
- The energy you put forth toward success is only to appear prosperous around people who do not grow you - those in your circle of limitation.
- You ignore all your financial obligations and you end up like most people with the sickness - *broke*.
- You purposely spend money as soon as you get it. It is almost as if you are subconsciously punishing yourself because you don't feel comfortable with large amounts of money.
- The only way for you to feel normal is to waste money on material things to mask how shallow you have become.

- The deeper the pain, the more expensive and glamorous you try to appear.
- Instead of finding the smartest way to use your money, you find the dumbest way to spend it.
- You begin to resent people with money; you feel jealous and threatened by people with cash flow.

Without money, you are fearful and dependent on those around you. You become a puppet held by the strings of those forced to support you. This causes you to slip into a state of low self-esteem and self-pity.

4. <u>Relationships</u>

- You only hang with people based on what you can get from them.
- Your relationships have no foundation, trust, loyalty, honor or respect to stand on.
- You screw over all the important people close to you and put on a front to all the people who do not mean anything to you.

5. <u>Time</u>

- You waste more time being the person you think other people want you to be than finding your own true self and purpose.
- You waste time giving energy to things that steal your joy.
- You begin to speak and focus more on the past than you do in the present or future.
- When you hear other people speak optimistically about their future you cringe on the outside, crack a half-smile,

- take a longer look at the ground or sky or you change the subject quickly.
- You become impatient and over-expectant of external things manifesting, but God's timing isn't at all a factor to you when it should be the only factor.

6. <u>Life</u>

- You have given so much energy into hating and sabotaging other people's lives that you have neglected your own.
- You wasted so much of your life gossiping and commenting on what somebody else did or didn't do right with their lives that you have lost creative control over your own.
- Your stress and self-hatred create an open window for people to see crystal clear into the part of your life you try to lie, fabricate and hide from everybody else.
- You suffer from a sense of belonging and worthiness.
- Your dreams turn into fantasies. Your life is driven by a fake reality which makes you hate your life even more.

7. <u>Swagger</u>

- You are only half the person you used to be. When you look in the mirror you still see the ghost of your old self and you want it back but it is gone.
- You live off the swagger of other people because yours is non-existent.
- You become a serial name-dropper, you mention the names of other people with swag, respect, and clout

whenever your credibility or identity is about to be compromised.
- You attach your name to solid people thinking you will receive the same treatment they do in life.

8. <u>Happiness</u>

- You become so depleted and miserable that you become isolated from the world and the overall joy of life.
- You look at life through a filter of spitefulness, guilt, and shame.
- You wish ill will on other people.
- Money, accomplishments, or admiration no longer bring you joy, nothing makes you happy not even love.

9. <u>Health</u>

- You feel like you are nothing or unattractive.
- You begin to care less and less about your appearance and more and more about what people who do not care about you think.
- You do not care what you take into your body, you go from treating your body like a temple to a trap house.
- Your energy is completely off balance.
- You are emotionally drained from all the stress.
- You are physically drained and lack motivation.
- You are spiritually drained because when you fall down you stay down and the devil is right there to use your circumstances as an excuse for you to believe God has forsaken you.

10. <u>Freedom</u>

- Your self-esteem is so low that you allow other people's opinions to shape and form how far you can go in life.
- You are kept in bondage trapped by the voices that tell you what you cannot do and you believe them.
- You can only be as bad or as successful as the suckers in your circle of limitation will allow you to be.
- You refuse to move past the circle that is blocking you from making it in life.
- You feel a false sense of loyalty to a group and a lifestyle that stunt your growth.

<u>Takeaways</u>

- ⌘ You are at war. The enemy is the devil. His soldiers are unclean spirits. The prize is your mind. What protocol do you have set for a response to an attack by an unclean spirit?
- ⌘ Identify the objectives of unclean spirits.
- ⌘ What are the different types of unclean spirits.
- ⌘ Who the author of all suckers is.
- ⌘ The problem is not the person but the spirits occupying that vessel.

ACTION PLAN

Examine the fruit of a person's spirit, listen past the words between the emotions towards the intent behind the narrative of the rhetoric. To stay sucker free and preserve your energy, you must operate in a spirit of humility, righteousness, and discernment. Remember to not allow anyone to compromise your operational spirit on any level, period. This allows you to reject the spirit a person comes in and not the individual. This spiritual separation is required for elevation.

Chapter Three

THE CIRCLE OF LIMITATION

The circle of limitation is any group of individuals you surround yourself with that limit the growth of life, self, and purpose. They limit you because they occupy the space and energy reserved in your life for the people who can uplift and develop you intellectually, economically, spiritually, socially, and emotionally, further blocking you from realizing your true purpose in life.

This circle has three dimensions:

1st <u>Individuals</u> in this circle.

They limit you in 5 ways:

- Intellectually
- Economically
- Spiritually
- Socially
- Emotionally

2nd Environment inside this circle.

This circle limits you by functioning as a comfort zone that leads you to one of three stages:

- First Stage - Rock Bottom
- Second Stage - Prison
- Third Stage - Death

3rd <u>Consequences</u> of being in this circle.

1. When you live life with no consequences you live life with no order.
2. When you live life with no order you live life with no structure.
3. When you live life with no structure you become a slave to your own desires.
4. When you become a slave to your own desires you develop a misplaced faith.

First Dimension: Individuals

They limit you intellectually by failing to provide you with a positive influence or legacy to follow. Only wanting to drink and get high every day or risk your freedom to make money.

This circle could be made up of court cases, baby mommas, bullet wounds, stretch marks, big rims, dope slanging, gangbanging, dead homies, bad credit, block stars, prostitutes, babies with women we don't love, different men around our kids, baby daddies or boyfriends either on their way to or from prison, Section 8, unemployment, student loans, and parole officers.

THE ART OF SUCKER DUCKIN

Many people in this circle have nothing to lose. They do not care if you live or die. That is all the more reason for them to ruin you. You have no direction or any righteous footsteps to follow in which leaves you potentially with no purpose.

More men fail through lack of purpose than lack of talent.

-Billy Sunday

They limit you economically by never teaching you financial literacy. You are not taught how to save, invest, or how to build credit, only how to spend. It's how to get it by any means necessary. This causes you to only be groomed to hustle one-dimensionally. You are willing to risk your freedom, raising your children, and your life just to get money. With the lack of entrepreneurial influence, you are only groomed for survival *inside* the circle, but you have no knowledge of financial survival in the real world.

They limit you spiritually and without realizing it, you put limitations on everybody and everything even God. Without God, you realize exactly how limited you are. You feel like you have limited options, opportunities, education, resources, faith, knowledge, movement, legacy, and vision. You become too self-absorbed and too ego-driven to accept any form of a power greater than yourself. You use your current lifestyle as an excuse for spiritual rejection. You will say, "I believe in God but the way I am living right now I cannot go to church because I am still sinning." This keeps you further trapped in the circle.

They limit you socially by displaying unhealthy boundaries because of the void of not feeling loved and never letting anyone get too close. You put up walls that block positive influences and welcome suckers. You take on a role in this circle; that role provides you with a sense of belonging and closeness to the suckers in this group who care nothing about you.

There is a role you play in the circle and then there is you. The role you play in the circle becomes an emotional camouflage to help disguise the pain you cannot express because you have no intimate or cohesive outlet. The more energy you put into your role the more it becomes your identity, which causes you to take on a personality of nothingness that dictates who you are.

Being around so many people you cannot trust, you begin to think the whole world is untrustworthy. This keeps you from meeting new people, and being loyal to people who betrayed you over and over again. This causes you to feel uncomfortable outside the circle because you think the world is the same as your circle.

In my circle, it was gang banging and dope slanging. This caused me to only associate with people who were truly entrenched in the same lifestyle as me. This caused me to not

trust anybody outside the circle or in it. I never allowed new people in because the circle was all I knew and that was what limited me. I never ventured past that circle.

I did not have a father figure so I joined a gang to feel loved and respected. I have been shot, been robbed, and sold drugs. I risked my life and freedom fighting over streets that did not belong to me and stayed loyal to a circle that cared nothing about me.

They limit you emotionally by grooming you to be led by pride and ego versus being in tune with your true self. The only feelings you know are happy, sad, and angry. You become confused by what you *know* vs. what you *feel*. You become a slave to your own desires and fears. Your emotional intelligence is low; meaning you are unable to empathize with a perspective that is different from your own. You have very little self-control, self-awareness, or sensitivity to the feelings of other people because the circle has made you numb to life. You lack persistence, self-motivation, and you are not shown how to properly interpret your emotions. You are only taught to show happiness or anger, but never shown how to function through hurt, pain, or resentment. Therefore, you get better at masking and bottling it up. Unresolved tension will always inadvertently lead to failure because it will always erupt at the wrong time.

Second Dimension: Environment

Once you have adapted to this circle, it begins to function as a _comfort zone._ Once in your comfort zone, the environment inside this circle of limitation will guide you to one of three places:

1. **Rock bottom**
2. **Prison**
3. **Death**

The environment inside the circle can come in the form of your job, school, neighborhood, church, family, friends, or relationship. Inside this circle, there is no encouragement, no support, and no uplifting of one another. Once in the vicinity of so many variables designed to stunt your growth like hate, crime, gangs, drugs, poverty, violence, racism, and nothingness you tend not to realize the totality of all the negative habits you absorbed by being in this circle.

It is amazing how people can make "nothing" seem so desirable. Material possessions, brand names and fast money are nothing more than appearance with no substance. One question I have is what is the purpose of risking your freedom to get money if you are not out to enjoy it with your family?

The environment when you hit rock bottom: Everything you have built begins to sink like quicksand. People treat you differently; instead of being supportive they conjure up intricate plots on how to use your current situation against you for their own personal benefit. No one understands you, people begin to speak to you with a disconnect. All the people you looked out for are nowhere to be found because they either stabbed you in the back or left you stuck because you are down.

The environment when you hit prison: is a completely different world; a negative hate-filled terrain plagued with tension infested with spite and driven by pure hopelessness.

Prison is a sucker's paradise; a land of powerlessness with zero control over the dismembered mirage of the old you and the world you used to know.

All of your material possessions mean absolutely nothing when you go to prison. The only thing you carry in with you is the same self-sabotaging mentality and reputation that brought you to prison in the first place.

Many, while in prison, fail to recognize the correlation between the circle of limitation *inside* prison versus the one they just left *outside* of prison.

If you do not strive to change your thinking while you are in prison, your incarceration can become a comfort zone. If this happens and you are eventually released, you will have a penitentiary prerequisite mentality. You will continually gravitate towards the suckers inside your comfort zone because that is what you have become accustomed to.

Due to my past way of thinking from my environment I lost my home, job, and a good woman.

The environment inside your comfort zone can lead you to an early death.

How many people have lost their lives simply due to the environment they indulged in? How many people have died as a result of just being a product of their environment? They join the gang because all the other kids in the neighborhood did the same thing and then they lose their lives. How many innocent people have lost their lives because they were in the wrong place at the wrong time? How many young black men have gotten racially profiled, pulled over and beat or killed? Or how many people have taken their own lives because they were not in an environment where they felt like life was worth living for? Say a prayer for those who fell victim to their environments.

Third Dimension: Consequences

After operating inside the circle of limitation you will have unknowingly been groomed to function and live without any care for consequences.

When you live life with no consequences, you live life with no order.

Living off impulse rather than instinct with no planning, no prioritizing, or challenging yourself, your life becomes a scrambled portrait of all you haven't done. Everything you were forced to do and some things you know you need to do, but deep down you are afraid of how your circle will receive you.

When you live life with no order, you live life with no structure.

No disciplined approach to life, just faint thoughts and flashes of what you were told *not* to do, and not what *to* do and why. Your decision making is led more by ego than intellect. Temptation outweighs the repercussions of ignoring the governing principles you were taught throughout life.

Trust in the Lord with all your heart and lean not on your own understanding in all your ways acknowledge Him and He shall direct your paths.

-Proverbs 3:5-6

When you live life with no structure you become a slave to your own desires.

You chase what you lust for not what you love. You entertain meaningless wants and procrastinate over necessities. You ignore your passion and pursue fleshly desires like gambling, drug abuse, overeating, or just becoming a slave to pleasure (Hedonism).

THE ART OF SUCKER DUCKIN

When you become a slave to your own desires you develop a misplaced faith.

You begin to indulge in a euphoric cycle of idolatry placing more faith in suckers and material possessions than God. You also become overly dependent on others and self. You begin to idolize yourself and make yourself a false God. You remove God from the picture.

Suckers will convince you it's okay to be spiritually shallow and that it's normal to treat God not as a savior but as a spiritual sugar daddy. You only summon Him to get you out of a jam or to go over your wish list never praising Him or believing in Him.

The ASD teaches you to lessen the amount of nothingness in life, to disassociate yourself from the circle of **_limitation_** and form a circle of **_elevation_** meant to cause all growth and upliftment.

Takeaways

- ⌘ Do you honestly have people that limit you? Who are they?
- ⌘ Are you in the circle of limitation and just now realizing it?
- ⌘ Have you ever pushed away someone who wanted to help you?
- ⌘ Do you grow the people in your circle and do they grow you?
- ⌘ Have you put more energy into gossip or working towards your goals?
- ⌘ Can you honestly say you trust the people in your circle?

- ⌘ Have you ever wondered why you are stuck at the level you are at?
- ⌘ Are you stuck between who you were and who you are destined to be?
- ⌘ Have you honestly outgrown the people in your circle?
- ⌘ Have you put more energy into suckers or nothingness than you have your own children?

ACTION PLAN

Begin to be more selective with whom you spend your time with because that will ultimately shape your future.

Think, do the people in your circle push you closer towards your dream or further from it?

You should never "normalize" toxicity or dysfunction. Your circle is supposed to elevate you. A circle of limitation can only work with your permission and you being complicit to the complacency of your own downfall.

Stop lying to yourself! Be real with yourself. Stop honoring the people who do not grow you, and screwing over the people that try to help soar you.

Chapter Four

THE PSYCHOLOGY OF PURPOSE

The psychology of purpose examines what may be mentally interfering with your realization of purpose.

The Fear Of Identity

The fear of identity can cause you to feel alienated socially due to a lack of understanding of who you truly are. If you knew who you were in God's perspective, then you would operate at your full potential. It is the lack of identity that leaves room for doubt. That lack is what many try so hard to fill with material possessions, titles, or lavish facades. The real issue is that many of us are frightened to discover how powerful we could be at the core of our identity. We go our entire lives living vicariously through an identity that we feel is acceptable.

At this moment ask yourself the following:

Who are you without your material possessions? Take away the money, position, street affiliations, or gang ties. Without all of those, who are you? Take away your job, car, friends, and the fancy clothes. Stripped to the core; who are you really?

The discovery of self breeds fear. Fear equates to hurt. That hurt equals pain while pain equals suffering. That suffering equals depression, and depression creates a thirst for happiness. Which leads to the formation of the necessary illusion.

Necessary Illusion

This act transports one *out* of their previous state of isolation (reality) *into* a short-lived world of false deliverance (fake reality).

> ***God will never bless who you pretend to be.***
>
> ***-TD Jakes***

This illusion causes an effect we will discuss in the next segment.

The Separation Of Self

The more people avoid who they are by pretending to be someone else, the greater distance they create from their true selves. The distance between the false self and the true self is the space many call home--somewhere in the middle. The suppression of self, versus the exposure of self causes many to want to be embraced as someone you are and accepted as someone you have run from your entire life.

The act of living in comfort with a counterfeit identity causes the result in the next segment.

No True Knowledge Of Self

When you have no knowledge of self you take on the personality of the suckers around you. You gravitate towards negative projections. The kind of false imagery we see acted out on social media, music, and entertainment platforms. This creates a narrative that killing your own is acceptable. When none of it is.

The most severe pain that hinders people is the silent rejection of self, multiplied by the rejection of the masses, plus the fear of self-discovery; minus how little you know about self-equals never discovering your true purpose.

Never Discovering Your Purpose

When the realization of a lack of identity begins to manifest into a core belief, this belief then acts as a wall. This wall shields people from experiencing any level of success or purpose in life. Simply put, the more you believe you will never be anything, the lesser the possibility. This keeps people in a state of mediocre thought and achievement.

How long will you run from your purpose?

When you run from your purpose you often waste time doing things you are not good at instead of occupying that time with fulfilling your calling.

- ⌘ The truth of the matter is some of you want to be thugs but you are not good at it, how can you tell?

You keep getting shot, you are broke, cannot pay child support, you keep going to and from prison, cannot pass a drug test, cannot build credit, and cannot pass a background test.

- ⌘ Some of you are still gang banging and dope slangin but you are not good at it, how can you tell?

If you hustle just to buy chicken wings, cigarettes, a bottle, and some loud, but have no bail money and you are broke the next day; you are not good at it. You have to be more worried about getting caught lacking than living. You are killing people who look like you. When you go to prison, your girl leaves you, and the majority of the time she ends up with someone you know--just saying.

> ⌘ Some of you men want to act like fake pimps but you are not good at it, how do you know?

If you leave good women for fast lust, if the woman you live with wakes up and says leave--then you are homeless; you are not a man. When you only have money when she feels like giving you some, your success lies in her hands.

> ⌘ Some women continue to choose the same toxic type of men in relationships, how can you tell?

You are single in a relationship; together on two separate journeys. Emotionally disconnected--these toxic men keep you comfortable in mediocrity and are unsupportive of you achieving greatness. These types of men will only be comfortable with you on a level they can manipulate you on.

> ⌘ Some women give more of themselves to a bum boyfriend than they do to their own purpose; how can you tell?

You spend more time worrying about a man than your talent. You are so consumed with wasted energy you cannot begin to focus on positive energy. Some women let their education go to waste because they have looked to a man to define themself instead of God.

⌘ Some single mothers spend more energy using their child as a pawn to hurt the father than actually allowing the dad to be a parent to his child, how can you tell?

You are always bitter; you never have any meaningful friendships, you are undesirable and you never realize your true purpose because you are too busy fighting a surface battle with the childs' father, but it is really with yourself.

Running from ones purpose and true identity has created the ***necessary illusion***. With this necessary illusion one can seek refuge behind an alter ego in which we will refer to as the gorilla suit.

That Gorilla Suit Does Not Fit You!

The gorilla suit is an alter-ego. People use this as a defense mechanism like a ***necessary illusion*** to protect an idealized self-image. It is a false sense of identity that has caused countless individuals to lose their freedom, lives, or opportunities.

WHY DO PEOPLE WEAR THE GORILLA SUIT?

- Because people would rather be who they think is acceptable than be themselves.
- To avoid feelings of insecurity, weakness, or powerlessness in certain situations.
- They feel if they are not in control, then they are being controlled.
- To escape accountability for the wrong they have done in their lives or in others.

- When someone cannot express their anger or accept a difference of opinion.
- When someone is afraid to let anybody get too close due to past trust issues.
- When they think humility means being a punk or being stepped on.
- To look tough because they are afraid of what people will think of them.
- To manipulate and get their way.
- To use intimidation as a way to cover up the underlying fear they have.
- To put up a fight when they really do not want to fight.
- When something is bothering them, but their pride will not let them tell anyone.
- When their egos feel threatened or their character is assassinated.
- When people cannot take constructive criticism they feel attacked and get defensive.

THE GORILLA SUIT AND SELF

Is your ego acting as the separate entity inside you that's conspiring to kill everything righteous within your life? Are *you* your ego? Your ego is your sense of self-esteem or self importance, not you.

What role does your pride and ego play in how you interpret respect and how you feel people should treat you?

The gorilla suit or ego's main priority is to maintain control at all times. What the ego does not know is the more time you waste trying to chase control, the more it will elude you. The ego is hypersensitive, prideful, and jealous. The ego is always in constant fear of being exposed. The ego is weak and cannot handle disrespect, rejection, or the admission of wrongdoing. The ego always feels as if it is always under attack from unclear threats meaning the ego will start a fight in an empty room. The ego is overly paranoid and will create imaginary wars because it never feels like it is never good enough so it always has to prove itself.

Has your ego blocked the humility, remorse, and selflessness needed for you to mature into the person God called you to be? Are you so blind that your ego has taken your true self hostage and brainwashed you into thinking they're the same?

The ego keeps you starved of self. The more you don't know about who you really are at the core, the more the ego can keep you dependent on it. A strong ego leaves a weak spirit. Feed more of your spirit than your ego, which have you given the most energy to? Be real with yourself?

This gorilla suit has you so preoccupied with the external perception you have developed a shallow understanding of your internal substance. You will never discover who you are at the core of self while wearing the gorilla suit.

You may have outgrown your circle of limitation, friends, environments, and deep down you want to change your lifestyle. You are not against changing, your ego is. The ego knows it cannot coexist in the same vessel as a higher power. EGO means Edging God Out.

Why would you rather be loved for who you are not than hated for who you really are?

Through this process one becomes dependent on suckers to stroke this alter ego. Thus leading us to codependency, which is defined as a person with excessive emotional or psychological reliance on a partner.

Codependency

Some people are reliant on the dependence of suckers to make themselves feel complete.

What does codependency look like?

This is when you want and need someone around you to feel happy in an unhealthy way. You become a caretaker and an enabler. You attach yourself to a suckers need for you.

How can you tell you are codependent?

- Excessively worried about the other person's personal problems.
- Attached to someone living their lives through you.
- You get a rush off of people needing to use your swag.
- You react to the pain, problems, behavior, and lives of people to make yourself feel complete.
- You need a group of people around you to make yourself feel like you're better. You are emotionally dependent on controlling them and you're attracted to them wanting to be around you because it strokes your ego.
- You justify people being around you because you found a use for them. Are you any of these?

THE ART OF SUCKER DUCKIN

Takeaways

- ⌘ What can psychologically block your purpose?
- ⌘ What causes the fear of identity?
- ⌘ What causes the separation of self?
- ⌘ Why do people have no knowledge of self?
- ⌘ How do people spend time while running from their purpose?
- ⌘ What is a gorilla suit?
- ⌘ Do you have a codependence for suckers?

ACTION PLAN

Change requires mentality maintenance. Perform routine self-inventory and confront what is at the core of self sabotage. What is consuming you externally cannot be flushed out until you remove what is contaminating you internally. Sucker duckin will never work if you are not real with yourself. For some of you the biggest sucker you are duckin is staring at you in the mirror everyday. Pray and ask God to remove anything from your heart that is not in line with His Destiny and your life will change. I guarantee it.

Chapter Five

SUCKERIZM

By definition, SUCKERIZM is the artificial principles you live by when you operate in the lower nature of yourself, or in a biblical sense, **your fleshly nature.** This is what keeps you blind to who you are, what you are, where you are from, and who God called you to be.

When you operate in this lower nature of yourself there are four traps that come with that lifestyle. These traps block you from tapping into your true potential.

The Four Traps Of Suckerizm

1. The Culture.
2. The Miseducation.
3. The Seduction.
4. The Addiction.

Oftentimes we wonder why we cannot progress to the next level. We blame others, but what are *you* doing that is blocking you from experiencing what God has in store for you?

While operating in the flesh you are not led by the principles of God but by Suckerizm.

The Culture of Suckerizm

1. What does the <u>Culture</u> of suckerizm look like?

- Thinking you have to risk your freedom to make ends meet.
- Being taught to hate and kill your own kind.
- Birthing children and not taking responsibility to raise them.
- Thinking that poverty is normal.
- Thinking that spirituality is soft.
- Thinking it is cool to be drunk and/or high everyday.
- Thinking the only two options you have is death or prison.
- Thinking you can only be a victim or suspect.
- Thinking it is ok to leave your kids and take care of somebody else's.
- Not knowing the true history of your culture.
- Thinking prison is a rite of passage.

I was influenced by drug addicts, drug dealers, killers, rappers, gangs, hustlers, and pimps. The culture inside that circle of limitation was to get money; to look fly and ride clean. Trust no one; never snitch and fear no man. Live fast, die young; do what I want, get high as I want, and take whatever I want. Remain loyal to my mob and die for them. This was the culture of suckerizm I lived in when I operated in my lower nature.

I was so consumed with feeding my flesh, I honestly had no room for God. If your spirit does not draw you towards the kingdom of God then you will gravitate toward principles that are artificial. You may think the way you live and think are correct, but they may not be in Gods' eyes.

Works of the flesh are evident which are adultery, fornication, uncleanness, lewdness, idolatry, sorcery, hatred, contentions, jealousy, outbursts of wrath, selfish ambitions, dissensions, hearsay, envy, murder, drunkenness, revelries and the like of which I tell you beforehand just as I told you in the time past that those who practice such things will not inherit the kingdom of God.

-Galatians 5:19-21

The Miseducation Of Suckerizm

2. How can suckerizm <u>miseducate</u> you?

- It is all about me – Self-centeredness.
- Thinking school is for **lames.**
- Thinking that a gang identity is who you really are.
- It is more important to look like you have money than to actually have it.
- Legit money is for squares.
- I need to be a part of a gang to feel like I belong.
- There is no need for financial literacy.
- Dope slangin and gang banging is a part of being a man.

The flesh will manipulate you into believing you can straddle the fence by living righteous on one hand and pleasing the devil on the other.

After I was sent to prison, I blamed God. I said why would you want me here? My previous thought process led me to think I could ignore God my whole life. I did what I wanted to do, turned my back on him, prayed to him the few times when I was in a jam. I based my belief in him on whether or not he did what I wanted him to do. I didn't fully trust him, I wasn't loyal to him, and said I believed in him, however never showed it. I gave myself and suckers more energy than I did God.

You cannot be neutral in Gods' kingdom. It is foolish to think God will ignore our sin and it will go unpunished. God responds to sin by letting Satan guide certain situations to go left when we need them to go right. He allows circumstances to counter what we wanted to purify our motives and test our faith.

Whatever man sows that he will also reap. For he who sows to his flesh will of the flesh reap corruption but he who sows to the spirit will reap everlasting life. And let us not grow weary while doing good for in due season we shall reap if we do not lose heart.

-Galatians 6: 7 - 9

The Seduction Of Suckerizm

3. How can you be <u>seduced</u> by suckerizm?

- Fancy cars
- Fast money
- Guns
- Power
- Gangsterism
- Dope boy swag
- Bad boy good girl combo
- Jewels and material possessions

When you abandon all intellectual and spiritual morals your flesh begins to crave the worldly and bodily desires of your lower nature. Nothingness pleases you more than any godliness.

The appetite of your flesh is starving for attention, longing for greed, infatuated with personal gain, and has a particular lust for idols. Idols are whatever you put in front of God. You can actually make people and things into false gods by worshipping them. False gods can be things like money, power, nice cars, jewelry, drugs, material possessions, beautiful women, or even yourself.

Your flesh is drawn to status, instant gratification, position, and lifestyles. So think… What do you love or pay homage to?

Some of you have careers and good heads on your shoulders; but the seduction of the lifestyle has caused you to flirt with a world you are truly not entrenched in. You feel as long as someone in that lifestyle **needs** you; you are a part of it. Everybody wants to be a part of something until it is time to get shot, robbed, killed, or go to jail.

I was tempted by fast money and violence, I never broke the vows that I had made. All I ever wanted was a mansion, a couple of fancy cars, a bankroll, and a beautiful wife. Anything outside of that was square to me, and I didn't care what I had to do to get it as long as I got it.

The question is, can you pursue God with the same passion?

But all those who desire to be rich will fall into temptation and a snare and into many foolish and harmful lusts which drowned man in destruction and perdition. For the love of

THE ART OF SUCKER DUCKIN

money is the root of all kinds of evil for which some have strayed from the faith.

1st Timothy 6:9-10

The Addiction To Suckerizm

4. **How can suckerizm become <u>addictive</u>?**

- Develop a drug problem.
- Develop an addictive personality.
- Become addicted to illegal money.
- Become addicted to violence.
- Become addicted to nothingness.
- Women can become addicted to the wrong type of man.
- Men can become addicted to the wrong type of woman.
- Become addicted to your ego.
- Become addicted to lust.
- Become addicted to drama.

The flesh enslaves you to a specific type of lifestyle and stunts your growth; by keeping you in jail or from experiencing a better way of life. This lifestyle may sometimes create the impression that if you are in the system you only have two options if you cannot find a job:

Option 1: Let your kids starve.

Option 2: Sell drugs.

This particular lifestyle may cause you to think you only have two options if you want to survive in the game.

Option 1: Not carry a gun to defend yourself, knowing that you may encounter enemies who want to kill you on sight for all of your past wrongdoings; and risk being killed.

Option 2: Keep your gun on you for survival purposes and risk going to prison.

Many are caught up in this senseless cycle of drugs, violence, and being led by the blind.

Some say to leave the lifestyle… to just change. Leave the state you live in, but that's not an option for everybody. Change is not a bulletproof vest. Even if I change my life for the better, the people I've harmed or done wrong to won't care. If they pull a gun on me, it's the end of the line no matter what I say. They're going to pull the trigger either way.

Some say just get a job, keep trying but in the meantime, I can't let my kids starve so I'll sell drugs. It's the addiction to the lifestyle. I know people if they hit the lottery they would still buy kilos to sell. It's a self-destructive cycle.

After the judge hits you with 140 months for 1st-degree sales… can you still say it was worth it? Now, not only is your family suffering without you they have to try and support you and the kids because of your absence.

If you have kids or want a better life, you should use that as motivation to change your lifestyle for the better. If not, you have played yourself.

I've seen so many loved ones and close friends negatively impacted by unhealthy lifestyles. Due to their loyalty to drugs and guns. With so many people losing their lives or freedom over money, family or disrespect it is ultimately tied to their addiction to a certain lifestyle.

If you find yourself trapped in this type of lifestyle and you want to change; first you have to surrender yourself to God and His word. Next, with all your heart, give Him the same loyalty, energy, and devotion you gave to suckerizm. Transfer that same energy to the one who created you.

> ***Commit your works to the Lord and your thoughts will be established.***
>
> *Proverbs verse 16: 3*

Once you change what you expose yourself to, then your circle will begin to change. You will not want to take advice from people who don't run parallel to your purpose. Once your circle changes, so will your environment. You will begin to put Godliness over SUCKERIZM and **no weapon formed against you shall prosper.**

This is the reality; an ADDICTION to the lifestyle of drugs and guns have no place in a childs' life or your own. We will always say we do it for our kids until we get locked up. All the money and material things we pride ourselves with will never be able to replace the time we miss in a child's life when we are absent. This is why so many kids turn to the streets. No father figure due to them being lost in the lifestyle and being imprisoned. They end up practicing the same lifestyle as their fathers. The cycle continues if your kids do not know the heavenly Father. Be sure to let them know they have a father above all that will never steer them wrong or ever forsake them. Actively put his presence in their lives.

Takeaways

- ⌘ What is Suckerizm?
- ⌘ How does operating in your lower nature limit you?
- ⌘ What does the culture of suckerizm look like?
- ⌘ How can suckerizm miseducate you?
- ⌘ How can suckerizm seduce you?
- ⌘ Can suckerizm most certainly become an addiction?

ACTION PLAN

Suckerizim produces sucker behavior; period. It keeps suckers near you but more importantly, it blocks your purpose. If you think you can progress to the next level without God first, that may be why you have not. You need to know God--develop a relationship with a higher power or enhance the one you have.

This is the reason so many of our youth are being killed because we are living in our carnal nature with no guidance from God.

Chapter Six

HOW TO BE SUCKER-FREE IN FOUR STAGES

Here the ASD systematically orchestrates how to be sucker free in four stages. The detox, relapse, transition, and fruition stage.

1. The detox stage - teaches you how to set boundaries and detox from wasted energy and the Devil. Also how captivity can consume your capacity and hinder your capabilities.

2. The relapse stage - the struggle between the two natures; flesh and spirit.

3. The transition stage - the death of your outward man; the old you or your fleshly nature.

4. The fruition stage - the birth of the inward man; the new you, or who God called you to be in the spirit.

THE DETOX STAGE

- Why boundaries are important and how to set them.
- The trauma of wasted energy.
- The Devil and wasted energy.
- The captivity, capacity, and capabilities.

Why Are Boundaries So Important To Purpose?

Boundaries are personal guidelines you establish to demonstrate acceptable ways you prefer to be treated.

If suckers see you have weak boundaries, they will pillage through your life. This gives them free access to disrupt your purpose. Suckers get upset when you set boundaries because they can not transfer their negative energy toward you. They will forever run into a brick wall upon arrival.

Sometimes when God reveals his purpose for you and the path he wants you to take, other people will not understand it. That is because it's not for them. It is specifically tailor-made for you.

Remember to set boundaries that match the direction your life is headed. You do this so you can allow the positive energy to penetrate. Think "purpose preservation"--if you receive a vision, follow it. How long will you let people who don't care come near it. This is where your systematic sucker duckin begins.

How To Set Boundaries And Enforce Them

You have to map out a personal plan. How will you respond if these boundaries are violated? I cannot do it for you. You must ask yourself:

- How much-wasted energy will you tolerate?
- How much positive energy do you need to function?
- How much space do you have for wasted emotions, senseless arguments, or toxic relationships?
- How much time have you wasted already?

- How much more money can you waste on looking the part?
- What places will you not go to? What places will you go?
- You have to move differently when you have something to live for, but still stay persistent, humble, and take risks.
- Are these the type of people I want near my vision? Do they make my vision clearer or foggier?
- This is why you need God to direct your path. He will place the proper people in your life to mesh well with the direction HE is taking in your life.

Types Of Boundaries

Energy Boundary: I will not allow my positive energy to be drained to replenish someone else's negative energy. *What is the consequence of violating this boundary?*

Time Boundary: I will be mindful of how I spend my time. Who I spend it with, what I listen to, who I listen to will all be purpose led--both professionally and privately. I will place a value on my time and not waste it or anyone else's. This time will be considered an investment. I will no longer let suckers waste precious moments of my life.

The consequence of violating this boundary will be?

Emotional Boundary: I will not allow another person's toxicity level to contaminate my vibe.

I will not participate in conversations or situations that jeopardize my mental stability or peace of mind. I have the right to walk away, hang up, and/or remove myself from any dysfunctional atmosphere.

The consequence of violating this boundary will be?

Financial Boundaries: I will not spend myself broke, I will save and invest. My emotions and finances will be kept separate.

The consequences of violating this boundary will be?

Talent Boundaries: I will not allow the gift that God gave me to go to waste. Each day I will try to find a way to somehow cultivate my talent and glorify God.

The consequence of violating this boundary will be?

Relationship Boundaries: I will not engage in relationships that jeopardize my freedom, safety, spirituality or peace of mind. I will not tolerate being treated any less than I am worth.

The consequence of violating this boundary will be?

You may be wondering "how do I communicate these boundaries to people?" What if they get mad? What if I love the person? What if they are family?

What Do Boundaries Sound Like?

These are templates you could use to empathetically create boundaries without ruining a relationship. You can use this as a format or create your own. Just be intentional about your guidelines.

- That is just not what I am into anymore.
- I'll pass.
- I need to get myself together before I can be of benefit to someone else.

- Having a little me time self-care does not mean I am self-absorbed honestly, try it for yourself.
- Just plain out NO! No can be said in a nice way but be taken in a mean way. With all due respect, my answer is still no.
- I need time to work on me and I need space to do so.
- If you respect and love me you will respect that.
- I understand you are mad but this is what is best for me.
- This is the path I chose.
- I am doing what makes sense to me, not what makes you happy.
- This is not about you, it is about my destiny.
- I love you but I love myself more. I cannot allow someone who does not appreciate my vision to set my boundaries for me.
- I can love you and still have boundaries set in place, or I can love you from a distance.

The Trauma Of Wasted Energy

Weak boundaries lead to wasted energy, and wasted energy leads to trauma:

- It manipulates your temper.
- It can consume your day, attitude, and dominate your thoughts.
- It can kill your ambition and weaken your drive.
- It can cause you to ignore your potential.
- You will give energy to what brings you low.
- You become tension-driven versus vision-driven.
- You gravitate towards hate, rage, pain, and anger.

- It can break your spirit and steal your joy.
- It can make you argue, stress, and fight over nothing.
- It can rob you of your self-awareness.
- It can cloud your judgment and taint your reasoning.

If you are unable to identify wasted energy when it is presented to you, you will forever be held by puppet strings.

The Devil And Wasted Energy

Whenever you strive to do good, change, or work toward a goal, the devil will always send wasted energy your way. The trick is being able to identify and respond to it correctly. It happens in three phases.

1. <u>The Distraction</u>

The Devil will attack you by sending wasted energy to you. It will come in the form of a situation killing your vibe, wasting your time or petty arguments. You think the Devil is attacking *you* but he is really attacking your potential, your mission, and God's purpose for your life.

2. <u>The Reaction</u>

This is how you act towards the distraction. Here, you encounter fake energy. When you flip out, yell, or stop what you are doing you cause a huge <u>*reaction.*</u> The only problem is you have been blinded by a huge <u>*distraction.*</u> You waste your emotional and physical energy on a situation by your response to it. <u>***Train***</u> yourself not to <u>***drain***</u> yourself, that is the discipline. When you are drained you have been manipulated. If you have no energy for God's purpose the Devil will resurface to lead you into suckerizm.

3. <u>The Divide</u>

Your reaction was meant to separate you from your mission. Fake energy from the Devil will appear real, but you validate it based on your response to it. Observe what you are giving energy to--is it the situation or your mission? Wasted energy is a form of bondage. Working toward your purpose you are breaking the bondage and transitioning into God's calling. The Devil uses wasted energy as a tool to separate you from living your best life. The more time you waste on negative energy the greater the distance you put between you and your purpose.

Think of wasted energy as a contaminant. That contaminant can consume your capacity. Once your capacity is consumed that leads to the captivity. That captivity is what destroys your capabilities.

Remove the contaminants: the contaminants are the suckers, but the Devil is the author of suckerizm. Both should be removed.

Free yourself from captivity: the captivity is the wasted energy, time, talent, relationships, money, and emotion that confine you to not living your best life.

Create the capacity: with the suckers out of the way, you can see your path clearly. You have room to grow your potential.

Focus on your capabilities: with the necessary capacity created in your life, you can begin to focus. You can begin to tap into your multiple abilities. Sometimes surrounding yourself with suckers for so long can rob you of knowledge of self. You can forget how talented you are because the suckers have dimmed your glow. Now with a clear canvas of life, you can focus on your capabilities instead of your limitations.

The Devil will use circumstances to manipulate and enslave you while God uses circumstances to condition and build your faith. God and the Devil both see attacks as an opportunity to build or destroy you respectively.

When you are attacked, that means the Devil is fearful and nervous so he will send division. He sends division in relationships and opportunities to cause a spiritual disconnection.

The wasted energy is only the vessel he uses to divide you from your purpose. Wasted energy is designed to blind you, test you, and consume you.

How Do You Monitor Your Energy And Maneuver Past The Attacks?

1. When the distraction happens, remember God is always in control. Repeat it to yourself over and over.
2. Acknowledge how crafty, sneaky, cunning, vicious, and thirsty the father of all suckers the Devil really is.
3. Practice the ability to step outside not only yourself but the situation. Think with your energy, not your emotion and will it be worth it; is this a setup from the Devil?
4. Train your brain to know what wasted energy sounds and looks like. You are in this to win it.
5. Pay close attention to who and what you give your energy to. Who and what you listen to and who you allow close to you.

6. Remember in the midst of trials and tribulations, certain barriers and obstacles put before you is only God conditioning you for greatness.
7. Realize that as long as you are wasting energy on nothingness, you have no time to focus on your potential. Stop being so easily pulled in every direction. Stop feeling like you have to respond to every sign you see or rumor you hear. That is energy that could go to a new hustle, your kids, or bettering your relationship with your higher power.
8. Remember that first comes the attack, second distract, and it all depends on how you react.
9. If you give people the chance they will steal your energy each and every single time. Create borders to avoid this recurrence.
10. When your energy is wasted and you have nothing left for God it is because the devil has consumed your energy.

THE RELAPSE STAGE

- The struggle between your (outward man) of your flesh and the (inward man) of your spirit.
- The struggle between the two natures who you *used* to be, versus who you are *destined* to be.

The Struggle Between The Two Natures In The Relapse Stage

The outward man is who you see in the mirror. The inward man is who you have always known you could be; but you could not see in the mirror. The outward man is like a costume you wear every day, over and over again. It does not fit and you feel ashamed wearing it but the comfort is why you wear it. You are in your comfort zone when it is on you. People have gotten so used to seeing you in it they feel funny if they see you in anything else and so would you.

The inward man is like an expensive tailor-made suit that has a glow about it. That glow comes from the reflection of God shining through you. In order to experience what God has in store for you, certain things have to change. People are drawn to the glimmer of favor that shines upon you. For some odd reason, you take the suit off after you tried it on (speaking in a metaphorical sense). Why?

You have the energy, power, and influence to accomplish your wildest dreams. You can attain unimaginable success, so why not wear the suit that was tailor-made for you by God?

You do not put on the suit of your inward man because the price tag is too expensive. You look at it like window-shopping. You think you cannot afford it because it will cost you friends, your reputation and influence. It will cause persecution for a life that seems unattainable--so why go through the hassle? That is why it is easier to put on the costume of the outward man. Because deep down you do not think you can afford it. What you do not realize is that the suit of the inward man was paid for in full by God. All you have to do is walk in your purpose.

The struggle is not in what you've been through or what you're facing; the struggle is in what you are willing to sacrifice.

Look at the hefty price you paid by living in your outward man.

Think of the inward man as a uniform and the outward man as a costume.

Why not allow yourself to be awakened?

Why walk in the darkness when there is light?

The more you continue to ignore your inward man, the more you will live a life void of purpose. Your purpose can not be reached wearing the outward costume of the flesh. If you want to fit in with the world, walk in your outward man. Do not continue to be another face in the crowd. Instead, you can tap into the inward man of your spirit and change the world.

The struggle is in the sacrifice, submission, and suffering. Through the beautiful struggle, you gain sustenance. Through sacrifice and submission you gain spiritual stature and the suffering creates steadfastness.

So Why Am I Stuck Between Who I Used To Be And Who I Know God Called Me To Be?

1. Why do I keep relapsing back to the old me?

Why- You won't let the old you die. You refused to fully surrender to something bigger than you. You are more focused on what you have to lose then what you have to gain.

2. You do not see the instant benefit.

Why- Because your mind is set on an event vs a pilgrimage and you seek instant gratification.

3. You look at it as a change instead of growth. Evolving and changing are completely different.

Why- You want to change without a challenge. There are challenges involved in growth.

4. You have fake people around that hold you hostage to who you used to be.

Why- Suckers will never allow you to thrive because they will have less influence around your life.

5. You have anemic faith as TD Jakes puts it.

Why- More belief in ego, others, and in the past than God.

6. You have no plan for when adversity strikes.

Why- You think an attack is an abandonment by God when it is really an affirmation that he's making you stronger.

7. You do not want to put in the work.

Why- Taking on God's calling you will be tested; unproven faith is useless.

8. You have not positioned yourself in an environment that wants to see and help you grow spiritually.

Why- You are not building with people who listen, motivate, support and love you. You are surrounded by people who do not hold you up but press you down.

9. You do not know how to navigate the struggle between the outward and inward man.

Why- Because you have not yet learned how to let go and let God.

Is your inward light dim due to the darkness of your outward image blinding your spiritual vision? Once you decide to stay rooted and allow God to let your light shine down on the inside you will reflect and live like it on the outside.

You have to do something different because you know deep down that you have it in you. You want better and for some of us, it's either **change or die.** Think about it before it is too late.

THE TRANSITION STAGE

- This is where you begin to shed your outward man completely and the old you begins to fade
- Here is where you truly begin to find yourself. The more real you become to yourself the more fake everybody begins to appear.
- Once you have this blank canvas in your life, you **_must_** fill it with positive energy, people, and influence. This is where you will get tested the most.

Are you at a point in your life where you have outgrown, out thought, and outfought what has been killing you? If so, ask yourself what are you keeping on life support that is dead to you? Think about that for a second. In the transition stage you can not move forward in the present by living in the remains of your past. This will cheat you of the future you deserve. For some of us if we do not change soon we will die. But the new you cannot survive because you will not let the old you die.

It is a race to see who will die first- *you* **or the old you.**
WHAT YOU NEED TO SURVIVE THE TRANSITION STAGE

Begin to identify with what your true purpose is

TD Jakes said that if you cannot figure out your purpose, follow your passion. For your passion will lead you right into your purpose. Purpose provides direction.

Expose yourself to the right people

The people whom you associate with should reflect the direction you are going in life. They should speak to your inward man, not your previous outward man.

Self-control

Let's be clear; you will be tested. There is a new devil on every level. Your boundaries and personal discernment are key to your survival. You have the right to choose who can and can not get close to you. Understand you have something to lose so purpose preservation must guide how you move.

Faith

The opposite of fear. My Pastor Daniel McKizzie says, "If you're worrying, start praying, and if you have prayed, stop worrying." Never underestimate the power of prayer or the discipline of having blind faith. Believe.

Strive for Godliness over religious conduct

Religious behavior consists of outward actions. This is people trying to gain notoriety from "people" through a behavior adjustment. Godliness is when people can see God in you, not on you and your moves will reflect that.

Prayer

If you ask you shall receive, based on God's timing. If whatever you pray for is in God's will, nothing can stop it from manifesting.

Energy focus and time management

You have to run your life like a business. In business you have to separate assets from liabilities. Your time and energy are two of your most key assets. From this point forward treat anyone wasting either one as indirect thievery. Use them like investments then examine the return on your investment.

Commit your plans, vision, and purpose to God and he will bring them to fruition.

Love

Seek love not from people, nor from the world, but from your Father. Give Him the same unconditional unwavering love that you gave the suckers when you were entangled with them.

Humility

Humility is the opposite of pride. Once new doors begin to open up you can easily forget that. God put you in position to see His vision come to fruition be greatful.

THE FRUITION STAGE

This is where you accept your Higher Power as your personal savior and discover the key to life, self, and purpose. Here you begin a new chapter in your life with the rebirth of your inward man, now that your outward man of the flesh is behind you.

You submit and surrender. You believe and receive it. Confess your sins. Ask for forgiveness. Commit your life to God. Read and study his words. Pray radical and deep prayers. Seek him in all that you do.

The reason you could never discover what your true purpose is was because you kept trying to do it without God. You kept trying to do your will, not God's. You have to have this foundation.

Imagine what you would set out to accomplish if you "believed" wholeheartedly God was with you every step of the way.

What is The Key To Life, Self, and Purpose?

Life

Your life was given to be surrendered, devoted, and used by God. This is to fulfill His purpose with your life not your own.

Self

You are to put away the old outward man of the flesh in order to glow up. You glow up by allowing the reflection of God's image to reflect through your actions. Put on the new inward man of the spirit geared towards God's instruction and likeness. Knowledge of self comes through being an imitator of the Lord and mirroring the character of the most high.

Purpose

God made you for his purpose not your own. You each have a gift specifically given to you by God. Once you allow Him to use you for His will, your life will ultimately change. You will discover your true purpose, living your life through and for God first.

Without God, you can never experience your true potential. You had to confront your fleshly nature then you had to examine your spiritual maturity.

I want you to go from being a people pleaser to a God pleaser.

I want you to be both fearless and unapologetic about God. I want you to stop being ashamed to boast about God.

Real men pray and believe in God.

Real women pray and believe in God.

A real man knows they are not perfect and that no one is perfect except God. Who have you been more loyal to--your plug or your God? Have you glorified the gift more than the giver? By placing God first and building with a Godly mindset, you will have a far better life.

Takeaways

- ⌘ How do you set boundaries and why?
- ⌘ How do you deal with the Devil and wasted energy?
- ⌘ What's the difference between the outward man vs the inward man?
- ⌘ What is the point of the transition stage?
- ⌘ What is the object of the fruition stage?

ACTION PLAN

I challenge you to live a life devoted to God. I challenge you to take off the suit of the outward man and step into your inward man. I challenge you to have a sucker free spirit. I challenge you to sucker duck from within. You will never be successful without boundaries. Set them, enforce them, put them ahead of other people's happiness. Think of your boundaries as the foundation of your self-actualization.

Chapter Seven

HOW WOMEN CAN BE SUCKER FREE IN RELATIONSHIPS

The ASD examines how a woman's most intimate alliance can block God's calling, shatter your inner peace, and slow your progress.

Women, are you single or sucker free? Is the relationship you are in slowing or growing you? Do you lie in bed next to your lover and still feel alone? Does the fear of starting over outweigh the unhappiness of moving forward? Is your attraction really your distraction? Has the wasted energy consumed your entire identity? Has your loyalty become slavery? Have you ignored your dreams to co-exist in someone else's nightmare? Are you giving life to the very thing that's killing you? Are you going to be unsuccessful and have a bad relationship or successful and sucker free? Can you sense the presence of God anywhere on your soulmate? Has people-pleasing left you dissatisfied? Do you know your worth in the relationship?

Know your worth before you enter a relationship

Oftentimes a woman will take a man with nothing thinking she can build him up. A man who's a sucker loves only himself and will define love based on how much he can *take* from a woman. Women know your worth. Know that it is not based on how much someone can take from you, primarily because when you stop giving a sucker will be gone.

What women should know:

- A man can easily fall in love with what you <u>do</u> not you <u>personally.</u>
- A relationship built on giving will never last.
- Know what needs you are trying to address before entering into a relationship.
- If he cheated, it was not okay. If you take him back, realize people can change. Remember, don't <u>lust</u> with a person you can't <u>trust.</u>
- Never allow a man to depreciate your worth.
- When you know your worth you won't stand to be treated as anything less.

If you are a woman who gives, set boundaries.

A woman who gives excessively in a relationship will sacrifice so much for the man she loves. All in hopes that he will reciprocate the same level of love back one day. The only problem is many men don't love themselves, but women don't realize it. Some women confuse arrogance with confidence or being manish with being a man.

So she feels the more she gives and the more he takes, the more he loves her and the more she's worth. A woman will give her heart, money, time, trust, love, home, and vulnerability to a man. Giving all this while receiving nothing in return she doesn't realize she's given away her identity.

THE ART OF SUCKER DUCKIN

What women should know:

- Women need to be careful to never give more than you are willing to lose in a relationship.
- Most women, when they love, they love wholeheartedly, but with a sucker all they do is take.
- Don't give to the point you are feeling drained financially or emotionally.
- It's okay to pour into someone, but leave yourself enough fluid to regenerate yourself.

When you give yourself to a man, keep your identity and set boundaries.

Have you given so much of yourself you have lost yourself? You can tell because you will search for your identity in the form of a man; who doesn't love himself. Have you loved your man to the point you have given him everything? Your power, happiness, and peace of mind? Have all these been siphoned away by a man? A sucker measures love for himself and for his woman based on how much he can gain from her.

Women what you should know:

- A man who loves himself and loves you as his woman will build you up when you are torn down.
- He will treat you as a reflection of himself.
- A real man protects, provides, and guides.
- Never love a man more than you love God.
- Always hold onto your identity.

Be secure with self first

A sucker will cheat, lie, take, then call you crazy and treat you like you're insecure. This is based on their negative appraisal of themselves. Remember, you are not dealing with a regular man, this is someone ultimately conspiring to kill everything righteous. What is righteous to him is your security of self. Never forget that. It is honestly a suckers' own insecurities that force them to keep your self-esteem low. They know with low self-esteem, it's easier to manipulate you. Men who are suckers in relationships maintain it by making the woman feel low or inadequate; mainly because that's how they feel about themselves. They secretly NEVER want you to reach your true potential as a woman because they feel you'll leave them for a real man.

Women, what you need to know:

- Your overall happiness of self has to come from self.
- Never let a man bring you so low to the point you begin to "think and act" as if you are the person he is portraying you to be.
- Know who you are before you enter the relationship.
- Know who you are with God first.
- You need to have a boundary in place for self-love for yourself.

Self-love vs sucker-love

Self-love is the regard for one's own well-being and happiness. Sucker-love is similar to narcissism take, take, and take. A sucker can have you intimidated just to exercise self-love in a relationship. Never interpret being used as being loved. Being in a relationship you are going to be used, but not to the extent a sucker will use you. Similar to a narcissist the more love you give them the more they will want to take.

Women, what you need to know:

- Self-love will give you the operating boundaries to communicate to a person how you should be treated in a relationship.
- Self-love is not a crime, most suckers have no love of self, they are just self-absorbed that's why they resent self-love for other people. It's a sign of a boundary.
- A person draining you for everything is a sucker not a man.

A Message To Women Who Keep Dating Suckers

- Stop dating people who block your blessings.
- Stop placing someone else in charge of making you happy. Your significant other can make you feel good, but happiness is an inside job.
- Never think sex is a security deposit on a relationship.
- Stop loving without trusting and trusting without loving.
- Stop holding on to who you want a man to be and ignoring who he really is.
- Stop sacrificing your happiness to make a man happy. Begin indulging in self-care frequently.
- If a relationship feels like prison remember you always have an outdate.
- If you are with a thug, gangster, or a drug dealer, just know jail is a part of the package deal.
- If you are past 30, do not beat yourself up if you are not married.

- Never be in love with a lie to save your pride.
- Be aware that a sucker can be resentful of your success and destroy you emotionally, financially, and physically.
- Define what needs you are trying to address before entering into a new relationship.
- Define what needs you can provide.
- Realize what your boundaries are.
- Do not jump into a new relationship following a toxic one. Most times part of you is still in that previous situation. Give yourself time to heal, evaluate, and conceptualize what went wrong and right. Relationship residue can be difficult for some.
- Only knowing what you want in a relationship is not enough. What are your deal breakers?
- Look for spiritual energy instead of material foolery. Never dumb down your vision for a blind man in his comfort zone.
- Never love anyone more than God.
- Never submit to a man who cannot submit to God.
- Find someone who speaks to the Queen in you.
- Is what you are attracted to distracting you?
- Understand the difference between the real and the prototype.
- Feelings are not facts, love yourself first.
- Love does not ensure obediance nor gratitude.

Ladies - How Do You Spot A Man Who's A Sucker?

- He does not take care of his kids.
- More worried about chasing women than purpose
- All he does is get drunk and high and lay around the house.
- Has no identity besides his woman.
- Always cheats.
- Will never let you move onto another relationship after it's over.
- Takes your money then goes and shows off to thots like he is a baller.
- Big ego, weak spirit.
- He is self-centered.
- He will lay up and play daddy to another woman's kids, but not his own.
- He wants to live off you.
- Insecure sexually, financially, intellectually, and never appreciates a good woman.
- He indirectly sabotages your stability with inconsistency.
- Never takes care of the home, but needs a place to stay.
- Puts himself before the kids.
- Creates more kids than he can take care of.
- He beats you.
- He keeps negative energy flowing.
- He is a narcissist at heart.
- He does not want you to win.
- Does not grow you, but slows you.
- In your circle, but not in your corner.
- Lies over stupid stuff.

- Blames everyone but himself.
- He is a hobo-sexual, a man having sex with you just to have a place to live.

Takeaways

- Why as a woman you should know your worth *before* you enter into a relationship.
- When giving have a limit in a relationship because suckers will bleed you dry.
- Be secure with yourself first.
- Know the difference between self-love vs sucker-love.
- How do you spot a sucker in a relationship?

ACTION PLAN

If the partner you are with fell into these categories then it is time to re-evaluate some things. The criteria by which you choose your mate from may be your downfall. Your attraction can lead to distraction. Start thinking long-term. What looks good for a second may not last forever. Just because someone desires you does not mean they deserve you. Learn to love someone, but learn to love you first. Set your boundaries, and do not compromise yourself.

Chapter Eight

THINK LEGACY, SPEAK DESTINY, GLORIFY YOUR CREATOR

No longer will you make small plans. No longer will you speak defeat. No longer will you magnify your limitations. This is the point in your life where you begin to focus on your God-given talents and use them to work toward who you were called to be.

Think Legacy

Before you build your new circle of elevation in place of your previous circle of limitation you need to always think legacy. When you consider your occupation, partnership, vision, or character, think how you want to be remembered. Consider your example for your children and how you glorify God. Always think about legacy. Think generationally with wealth,--what do you want to leave your childrens' children?

Being legacy-orientated gives you a sense of vision bigger than you could've ever imagined ask yourself:

How do you want to be remembered by the world, society, community, family, and friends?

I want you to answer these questions on a piece of paper and hang it on your wall. It sets the tone for the path you choose to walk. Just ask the creator which way to go and He will ultimately be your guiding light.

Being legacy orientated transforms your narrative. Everything you do must be in some way harmoniously connected to the transitional thumbprint you want to leave on this planet.

Speak Destiny

You have to make it a habit of speaking things into existence! If you are a winner, claim it! Speak it! If you plan to be rich, speak it! What you say attracts who comes around and who doesn't. Certain people will know they can't come to you with petty talk only kingdom talk, nation building, or community restoration. Begin to speak your destiny outward toward the universe and boldly live it inwardly even if you are the only one it makes sense to. Pray and you will begin to attract the necessary pieces to the puzzle needed to fulfill God's plan.

<u>In order for you to manifest destiny you have to speak it!</u>

Tell yourself you can have it. Believe you can achieve it. Then go humbly and persistently in the direction towards it. Grab it. Speak life into your purpose with intention and never SPEAK DEFEAT! Have **Destiny Dialogue** with your creator and yourself daily. Claim what your creator has already laid out for you.

Glorify Your Creator

Now that you are free from the captivity of nothingness, suckers, wasted energy, and a circle of limitation, you now have the *capacity* to glorify your creator. When your blessings begin to come never be fooled and think it's all about you. Always glorify

God in every stage of your life. You glorify your creator by using what God has blessed you with to help benefit and uplift His kingdom.

Success can cause some of us to become proud or egotistical in other areas of our journey. If you keep God first and most importantly trust him, you will never fail. He will never put on you more than you can handle. Praise Him in the good and the bad. Thank Him for the new chapter you are about to embark upon.

Takeaways

- ⌘ Being legacy orientated is the foundation of purpose preservation. This mentality will shape your conversation and highlight your destination.
- ⌘ Speak destiny (self-talk) what you say matters, speak life over your circumstances, and pray for guidance.
- ⌘ Think legacy by creating generational wealth for your childrens' children. Create generational opportunities and break generational curses within your family. How do you want to be remembered and why?

ACTION PLAN

Be intentional about the mark you leave on this earth. Be active in your family, effective in your community, and influential in society. You can have more degrees than a thermometer, but if you are not using them to uplift God's people then what is the point.

Destiny dialogue, practice speaking victory in the face of adversity say out loud "I CAN." Speak boldly towards success and mighty toward uncertainty in the end just know you are worthy.

Don't get so lost in the blessing that you forget who blessed you. Practice glorifying your Creator every chance you get. God blessed you with a gift now use it to bless Him and those who need it.

Chapter Nine

HOW TO BUILD A CIRCLE OF ELEVATION

Cultivate capabilities

How to build a circle of elevation (COE).

A circle of elevation is a group of individuals that uplift you economically, emotionally, spiritually, socially, and intellectually. This is how you structure your COE:

- **1st - your nucleus**
- **2nd - inner circle**
- **3rd - outer circle**

The Nucleus

It starts with you and God, this must be the nucleus of your circle.

Between these layers, there is a boundary.

- Your relationship with God comes 1st.
- When God is at the center of the circle it sets the precedent.
- If God isn't at the center of your life you are set to fail no matter what.

- There must be a boundary between you and God and your inner circle.
- The key to this maintaining relationship:
- Vulnerability
- Communication
- Consistency
- Accountability
- Trust
- Belief

The Inner-Circle

Your inner circle must be carefully selected with extreme caution. These should be primarily family, close friends, or friends that may be closer than family. These are people who uplift you, the caliber of pedigree should be purpose driven with infinite vision.

Intellectually: They build you, they appreciate and stimulate you on so many levels. They teach you, correct you and hold you accountable. They also speak life into you when you feel dead to the world. You can be vulnerable with them because they want you to win and can wake up the visionary inside you. They value your presence, have intelligent conversations, and bring out the best in you. They make you smarter; the true definition of an asset.

Economically: You can trust them with money, but they can also show you different ways on how to grow your money. For example, cooperative economics, group economics, and financial literacy. They want to make money with you, not steal it from you. They can create and inspire the entrepreneur within you, unlike the suckers who simply take and destroy.

THE ART OF SUCKER DUCKIN

Spiritually: They speak to your spirit as if you were kindred. They pray with you and for you. They keep you spiritually grounded. I strongly suggest having spiritual mentors because we wrestle not against flesh, but against principalities. Also against powers, against the rulers of darkness of this world, against wickedness in high places.

Socially: They uplift your network and grow your net worth. They grow you in a cultural and societal aspect. Your peers become more aligned with righteousness and success so much that you begin to normalize happiness and become the asset you're seeking from other people.

Emotionally: They provide motivation, energy, confidence, and the purpose needed to help carry you to the next level. They exercise emotional intelligence by displaying self-awareness, motivation, and empathy. They manage their own emotions and maintain a healthy relationship with you.

Between these layers, there is a boundary.

- Define who these people are.
- Cherish every moment with these people.
- Don't bring the same type of energy you had with suckers to this crowd.

There must be a boundary between your inner circle and the outer circle why? Because your inner circle is where you're most vulnerable. This is why the safety and well-being of your loved ones are first, not just anybody deserves access to this. This is how the suckers were able to penetrate so easily and have such a negative impact on your life, they had **ACCESS.** This is why toxic relationships have such an adverse impact on your success and purpose. Hold this inner circle sacred.

The Keys to Maintaining Your Inner Circle:

- Appreciation
- Communication
- Respect
- Trust
- Compromise
- Honesty
- Love

The Outer-Circle

Your outer circle should be structured as a cabinet of advisors and mentors. This is the infrastructure of your outer circle. These should be your professional relationships. Mentors in business or the industry you are interested in planting your flag. Support this layer of your circle tremendously. Always build, share projects, and ideas with these people. Take criticism and advice. Give the same amount of loyalty and energy to this circle as you did that circle of limitation and you'll be fine. Learn, love, and bless this circle. Win-win should be your mentality.

Between these layers, there is a boundary.

- Define who these people are.
- With this circle, remember to think legacy, speak destiny, and glorify the creator.
- These people are vital to you and you must make yourself valuable to them.

There must be a boundary between your outer circle and your circumference. Be very cautious when allowing access between layers it's up to your discretion.

The hard thing about everyone in your outer layer is they're not necessarily your friend. Just because someone supports your venture or believes in your product doesn't necessarily mean they're your friend. Know the difference between friends and business associates. Some may just be along just to ride the wave. Be sure to be a solid friend though and always have a keen sense of who falls in what category and why.

The Key to Maintaining Your Outer Circle:

- Support
- Networking
- Timing
- Sacrifice
- Time
- Compatibility
- Longevity

The Circumference

These are the people who are on the outer layer of your outer circle. You hardly ever see them if at all and when you do it's rare, but the love and respect are still there. Just a different type of love, a different type of access, and different types of interactions. These may be the people whom you may have to love from a distance; or appreciate from a distance for whatever reason you know who these people are.

The boundary.

- Define who these people are.
- They may not necessarily be in tune with your purpose.
- You may only have a digital relationship with them.

The most important thing to remember about this circle is that this one has boundaries. I don't recommend cross-pollinating every layer with the next. You control when and if ever these layers should meet. This will keep you on a path of purpose preservation and keep you sucker free.

The Key to maintaining your circumference:

- Loving from a distance
- Discernment
- Respect up-close
- Common values

Takeaways

⌘ Why is it important that you keep God at the center of your circle?

⌘ How and why is it important for people to grow you intellectually? As well as you grow them?

⌘ Who belongs at the circumference of your COE.

⌘ Why is it important to have boundaries of layered insulation within and around your circle?

⌘ Boundaries are the reason you removed your circle of limitation to create this circle.

- ⌘ Your happiness in life is honestly based on the closest influences around you.
- ⌘ What will you do to maintain this new circle you have?

ACTION PLAN

When making the decision of who to give access to your circle; don't be careless with it. Don't use the same criteria as before. This is your life, fill it with people who make you better. Many people make the mistake of thinking once they have created a new life they can bring old suckers into what they newly built. Select wisely. Always place people in your circle you want to win and visa versa. Push them to strive and do better. Keep your circle central to your success, trust, build, be a lifelong learner, and you will remain sucker free!

THE ART OF SUCKER DUCKIN

BY: TIERRE CALDWELL

Relationships matter. When you pick your friends, you pick your future. If I want to know who you are, I can look to who you run with. I wrote this book because I was tired of seeing people get killed, thrown in cages for life, and powerless over toxic relationships. Many know who God is, but not the Devil or their fleshly nature. I realized a lot of it has to do with who you associate yourself with.

While the whole world has been so fixated on "haters" a newer deadlier enemy has surfaced and managed to sabotage you in your inner circle without you even knowing it. Lying in bed with you, getting high with you, at work with you. Who are they, SUCKERS! A SUCKER is Someone Ultimately Conspiring to Kill Everything Righteous. DUCKIN stands for Demonstrating an Understanding of Conscious Knowledge Immune to Nothingness. The Art of Sucker Duckin.

About The Author

TIERRE CALDWELL is an employment navigator with a non profit, and is a member of the American Civil Liberties Union (ACLU) Smart Justice Advisory Board. He is a lead mentor for a youth development program and a frequent speaker with the Federal Community Outreach Program to students about drug prevention. Tierre is also an advocate for criminal justice and prison reform to end mass incarceration.

Tierre grew up with a phenomenal mother and sister. He had no positive male role model, only the street. He was shot in the head when he was 17 years old. Growing up he was impacted by the criminal justice system as a result of poor decisions and who he surrounded himself with. He lost countless friends and opportunities. Something had to change.

As he began to mature spiritually, he denounced his gang affiliation, and drug addiction. He can proudly profess that he has been sober in recovery for over 10 years strong.

He began to self educate, take college courses, write continuously, and study African history. He became dedicated to self-development. He partook in leadership training and it changed his life. He admired the training so vividly that he requested to stay on as a mentor of the teaching. He also saw an opportunity to use his life as a vessel. To help others find God, stay out of prison, out of gangs, off drugs, and surround themselves with people who want to win! Thus he began to write a self-help book called The Art of Sucker Duckin.

CPSIA information can be obtained
at www.ICGtesting.com
Printed in the USA
JSHW051733270623
43837JS00003B/221